canon

canon

mx jen durbent

No part of this work may be reproduced or transmitted in any form or by any means, electronic or mechanical, including by photocopying or recording, or by any information storage or retrieval system without the proper written permission of the copyright owner unless such copying is expressly permitted by federal copyright law. HYBRID Ink, LLC is authorized to grant permission for further uses of the work in this book. Permission must be obtained by the author or the publication house. Address requests for permission to make copies of material here to the email address hybrid+permissions@hybrid.ink

A previous version of "Ruins of a Memory Palace" appeared in I WANT TO SEE YOU BEFORE I LEAVE <https://www.beforeileavezine.com/jan-2018/toc>

ISBN: 978-1-948743-06-8

canon

Copyright © 2018 mx jen durbent
Cover illustration:
detail of *Las Palomas* by Daniel Hernández Morillo, public domain.

Publication: 3.0-print (First Edition), 2018.
All rights reserved.

HYBRID Ink, LLC
Independent Publishers of Thoughtful Writing

hybrid.ink
Everett, WA

Printed in the United States of America
10 9 8 7 6 5 4 3 2 1

On Her Existence (2018) 1

to break your own heart 5

Nolo Contendere 7

leap year 11

Flight of the Hippopotamus 15

flood 17

A Loving Myself Ghazal 19

bury me as a woman 21

the raft (2018) 23

Meaninglessness 25

Ruins of a Memory Palace (2018) 27

one deep breath away from weeping 31

Pagliacci 33

Haiku for My Fellow White People 37

Boketto 39

American Canon 41

The First Man I Loved 47

a dream of undoing 49

10 simple rules for dating a trans girl 53

LGBTQuisling 59

xenoglossia (2018 rev) 61

Storming the Foothills of Mount Olympus 75

Content Warning

Sexual Assault, ACAB, R-Slur, T-Slur, Violence, Drug Use

Our documents are useless, or forged beyond believing.
—The Church - *Destination*

For J.

On Her Existence (2018)

> *A poet more than thirty years old is simply an overgrown child.*
> — HL Mencken

Excuse me! Excuse me! Sorry to bother you while you're reading
your book, and I'm sorry if it's creepy,
but I can't help but notice that you put
non-dairy creamer in your fairly-traded,
organically-grown, coffee-shop coffee. Well, maybe that's not creepy.
But I'm pretty sure that it is creepy that I can't help but notice
the cut of your skirt, the height of your heels,
and you might want to pluck your eyebrows.

I'm not saying this as a judge , but you
might like to know. I just notice
even when if I can't look at myself in the mirror
and take my own advice. I don't want to say more
and I can't help myself and I know
you might be offended and I apologize. It might sound
weird coming from someone
that looks like I do
that I can't decide if I want you
or if I want to be you.

I know that it's not OK. I know you
are a fully formed person and that your presence is not
an invitation. My brain is limited.

These couple pounds of meat is no immovable
object against the unstoppable force of unwanted testosterone.

But I'm trying.

The latter might be more interesting, but it's grown difficult
to discuss, though I will try. I am afraid
I can't help it. Just remember when I say the light in my soul
went out: you had nothing to do with it.

Inside I have my own goddess and she is hope for proper gnosis.
Is it shame that I do not believe in her? I'm afraid
I can't help it. She is barely a breath, nearly invisible
like the steam off chai. I don't think I am being clear.
It's not really my fault; but it is.
I am afraid.

Let me just say it.
Part of me—part of this him—
is a her.
And I'll be damned if she isn't fabulous.
She comes out to say to the universe, "I exist."

But this him pushes her away with tears and
the iron and food and hate and says,
"Just wait, please." She is patient, but
she doesn't want to wait, not really. She is beyond waiting
and chastising me for edging into cowardice.
I can't blame her. Would you want to be trapped inside
this terrible visage? So I tell her:

CANON

"You should never want to be real.
Because the world is worse for hope;
because dreams never ever come true;
because dessert never is as sweet;
because fury never is as righteous;
because sex never is as dirty;
because crying never is enough release;
because love always is lopsided
because whoever gives less has more."

She doesn't believe me. At all. Logic cannot dissuade
her, especially when she's not constructed of logic;
she is the result of the mathematics of synapses, sinew, and hope.

Enough about me, or her, or us!
You inhabit your body, your poise
and your pose
and your placement of leg atop leg
and hand on handle
and the way you hold that book. I can see roots
in your dye job;
somehow that makes me envy you more.

So when I get up to leave, please remember as I pass homeless
teenagers warming their hands over unlit tinders: I do not stare
just because of lust (though I cannot deny that). I stare
because you are beautiful to the one sharing my heart and she
wants to ask you how you became
so beautiful, so real, so true.

to break your own heart

To break your own heart,
find a seam
previously mended
and place it on the edge
of a desk,
intended for great novels
but used to write
suicide notes.
Grip either side of your heart firmly,
as if this were murder
(because it is),
and
p u s h.
After the snap
tells you it's done,
mend the injury
with tears, ice cream.
Add a dose of silence
and compassion for her
because she never asked
for your love.

Nolo Contendere

for Zinnia Jones

I have transed
the boys
that were
on the internet

which
you were probably saving
for capitalism
and war.

Forgive me,
they are girls now,
so treat
them good and right.

They need love,
estrogen,
and blankets
because
they are sweet
and your world
is so cold.

the blind woman in love with medusa

Inspired by an illustration by Dahui Wang

Smell of the sea wafted through ruins
already ancient before we took up residence.
There was the warmth of the sun on the roof,
the singing songbirds, the occasional breeze
dimpled our skin.

There was me, Tiresias, a prophet. The gods
made me a woman, too. But I laughed. They think
womanhood a vile and horrible curse, but it is
a blessing. And there was my love, Medusa,
the serpent-haired beauty. Beauty? Those who saw
her turned to stone, such is the curse when glimpsing
her perfection. Trust my words; I know things that gods
keep secret. That is why I am blind: sight stolen by
small gods for a long forgotten slight.

We lived for years, her flesh soft and mine as well.
We lived as woman and woman. We lived with joy.
We lived with love. I knew her beauty, I felt the chill
of stone in my bones as my fingers traced her face
still warming my heart. Her kisses sweet to make
the finest fruits as rotten meat.

We both had needs, and I tended to hers.
I went to the market for her fruits: grapes

and pomegranate firm and ripe. I placed them
in my knapsack when I heard her screams.
I let my cane guide me homeward bound.
When I arrived, I found new pair of columns
made from men and my Medusa, my dearest,
without her head. Her beautiful voice, her touch,
her smell replaced by the rot and putrid stench
of a man's lust for glory.

I cried out, "Where are the righteous angels
who carry death in their purses? Why are
you not here for me?" I cried and the curse
washed out of my eyes and I could see
again and my first vision was the woman I loved
struck down. I wailed at the vision, so I scraped
out my own eyes and held her fast and tight.

I pray the vultures come quick and take
our bodies to heaven. Now I lay next to her.
I strike my own wrists with the sword of gold
and a wait for the end, for us to be together
again.

leap year

Shattered amber glass bottle shards
sparkle across the alley as stars.
(Sterne waren schöner,
als ich
ein Mädchen war.)
Discarded needles point up
like antennae to heaven.
Flowers bloom
in February sun and lilacs fear
no frost from our dying land.
We have stretched patience
and prudence
to cowardice,
as taffy pulled and pulled and turned
and stretched and then burned,
covering all the fields
in forgetful ash.

Two children play in front of a garage
The games are as before.
Forts
from coffee cups
once protested fiercely,
mended together
and measured out
with coffee stirrers.

JENDURBENT

The brown-haired one flicks
a marble
fast
and laughs as structures crumble.

Across the alley from them: a high-rise.
Built in some forgotten age and
carved from concrete and decorated with
more rotten pine-wood patches
than windows.

I turn down a road and find houses
made facades, only the front remains.
Through windows I see
sky where living rooms had been,
where Christmas trees held presents,
where hard discussions were had,
where quiet nights were spent in front of televisions.
Buildings stolen, mortar made mush
their bricks picked like vegetables
and shipped to artesian bricklayers
building behind gates with guards.

In Wetsoff's husband's words,
"Und nur der schweigsame Tod, der weiss, was wir
und was er immer gewinnt, wenn er uns leiht."

The past is gone,
that hostile foreign country.
I only remember

CANON

Sears Tower's shadow reaching into the lake,
antennae like a claw.
Last time we went
all there was were
dead gulls,
a sailboat shattered near a fallen pier,
and a tide way out.

Flight of the Hippopotamus

They flew in the food on Thursdays
until last week, when the plane went
down, smashed against the mountain
ridge, less than a mile from here.

You can see the burnt out skeleton
from the village's highest hill, over
the trees and against the granite,
decomposed, ashamed of nakedness.

Hopi, they say, is better suited to discuss
quantum mechanics than English.
Maybe that is true. Everything is
better said through other people's words.

But I do know that when we screamed
at the explosion in the sky like children,
my own voice was merely an
echo of everyone around me.

And, on the fourth day, the elders and I
passed a decomposed camel corpse,
on route to the plane to scavenge; all we
carried back were razors and burnt t-shirts.

JENDURBENT

The heavy-handed lesson of survival was:
I left on the sixth day. My plane came
from the west out of the sun. I flew
to the sunset, violent chrysalis behind me.

flood

    wish
        for
            the
        path of
            least
                resistance
            Lest
    we
let out feelings and they are too much for the dam to hold.

A Loving Myself Ghazal

> Write a poem, Jen, about all the reasons people rightly love you. I expect no less than 10.
> —Jenny V Simile

Unsure, a woman on a balance beam for first time in many nights.
I am to enumerate loves for me of all sorts, both by day and night.

I held him as his wife died. He looked at me with a heart wounded.
I held him in my heart and nursed him back from his soul's dark night.

A woman sees me with her esteem low, "At least I don't look like that," she says. Her laughter echoes through the night.

Looking up, her one uncovered eye a mix of lust and fear: grab her hair, point her face toward me, our kisses explosions in the night.

The mat sits in front of our door, covered in mud, mold, and dead leaves.
"Welcome," it says as she stands on it, fumbling with her keys every night.

"Mom," she says and looks at me. "It hurts." Me gentle hand on her tummy,
the cramps tightening until she sleeps. I stay with her all through the night.

If absence makes you grow fonder, then I will be the source of all
delight! My fears of being a burden, plans of leaving keep me up all
    night.

My mother says she loves me; she calls me and tells me I am a
    beautiful
girl. I hate it and don't know why. I still cry almost every goddamn
    night.

After a show, a trans sister gave me a hug, thanked me for
    performing,
for being visible, and she ran off with her friends ran into the night.

We held each other, our legs intertwined, our fingers interlaced, our
    lips
locked, the curtains pulled tight and drawn, making a facsimile of
    night.

The mirror is kind today! It reflects a proper color light; perhaps fat
has moved subtly. Now I see a Jen. I see a girl worth holding all night.

bury me as a woman

The ground
is the only thing
I trust
to hold me true
and hold me forever
as I am
and always will be.

the raft (2018)

It is hard to see
log lashed to log,
in the waning
moonlight.
The raft floats
on the open
sea.
Its tattered
sail pointing toward the past
like a monument.
The lone passenger—
oh captain—a girl standing
with red sun-bleached hair—
looks to the bow,
guiding herself
by the stars her father
taught her nigh half a world away.
Those same eternal lights
in the sky his father's
father taught his father
who taught
him.

JENDURBENT

The waves rise up
up and crash down but
her ship's close hauled sails
take her toward a place
she used to call
home.

Meaninglessness

A submarine sits, broken in half,
crossed akimbo on the sea floor;
the skeleton of an almost-survivor
is a floating home to fishes.
Coelacanth rests in the ribcage
of a once-man. Dinosaurs, evolution
of man: trivialities. In death
there is a use for this man;
before, he just took up space—
him and all his neighbors,
lovers, parents, and siblings.
An ancient fish thought extinct
doesn't concern itself with sunrise
after any solstice or white dunes
on the seafloor.

The skeleton is as unimportant
as the president; an artificial reef
bisects the hull with vicious colorless
barnacles.

These fish will see the sun boil
off the oceans as it grows larger
and reddens the sky. No-one will
ever catch him with a hook and lure,
shoved through the cheek.

Ruins of a Memory Palace (2018)

I don't memorize my poetry because
I don't trust my memory.
My memory does tricks like
"You coulda" and "You shoulda" and
"You asked for it."

I keep kind notes in my purse
I keep them safe.
I keep them so
I remember
people like me
people love me
my dog feels what dogs feel but
at least his tail wags, shedding hair
I will sweep up later.

Without the kind words
I just remember:
I hate you.
you're ugly.
nobody wants you.
you're retarded.

My memory does tricks:
when I see a cop, I remember
when I was 4, I was handcuffed
and laughed at and fingerprinted.

{ As an aside: this ruined bondage
until I discovered leather, latex,
and rope. }

When I smell pot, I remember
the man
who tainted
the joint that we smoked
and all the ones I
turned down after.

Despite my best efforts I do not
clearly
remember
the birth
of my children
and I don't know if that's because of my
awful, terrible, no good brain
or because I was the second most exhausted person
in the room, and
then the third.
[Do not tell them, not
like they would remember either.]

Texts from the woman
who says she hates me
once
are 1000x more in my memory
than the countless I love yous.

CANON

That part is true
that she tells me she loves me.
I wrote it down
just now
just so I would have something
to trust.

I hate my memory.
I hate scenes never forgotten
and those long gone.
My memory does tricks after all.
If you're too good to me,
it might make you disappear.

I feel as if I have lived two lives,
the first life with evidence,
what my notes say,
what loves,
what recommendations,
what money and therefore symbols that people give
when they say, "your words are worth something,"
and the other life of memory,
what I remember,
what I wish I could forget.

I might have missed the point here.

I meant to copy pasta, to trans scribe
the good parts of my life so I can't forget:
My daughter braiding my hair

Her helping me learn to
Wing the eyeliner just so.

[You can make over a tran
and she's cute for a night;
or you can teach her
and she can be style
her whole life.]

I meant to write the thank yous
that the kind words deserve
that the days I wake up and read them and
that gets me up and out of bed and through the day,
including this morning,
to read this to you.
Thank you all you bright and rising angels.

Despite what RuPaul
and the self-help books say,
I can love you.
I hate myself better than anyone
but I love you,
too.
And that I will never forget.

one deep breath away from weeping

One deep breath away from weeping we buy our pickles and salt.

One deep breath away from weeping at nothing at all.

One deep breath away from weeping, we decide to move forward and never stop.

Pagliacci

I have this joke
About when cops took me from my parents
when they cuffed me
What I leave unsaid is
I hyperventilate when I see men in uniform.
I do not feel safe when they are
anywhere. They are all dirty.
I don't finish that story
because who knows who is in the audience?
That thin blue line
encircles them all like a witch's ward,
the blue stripes on a racist flag for a country
promised hope and gifted horror.
Hashtag not all cops.

I have this joke
About how I do not want a vagina
Because I saw my wife
Give birth.
Twice.
I can't compete with that.
What I leave unsaid
Is
I cannot mother like that.
I cannot hold a child inside.
I cannot stand thee insides.

JENDURBENT

A baby will never call me "Mom."
I don't finish that story
Because they don't pay me to cry on stage.

I have this joke
about how Bible Thumpers
Told me I need a man.
I found it validating that
they saw me as a woman.
What I leave unsaid
is that when they called me ugly,
gross,
and all the rest.
I don't finish that story
because I need to project confidence,
even if what the preacher man
said was true.

I have this joke
about killing myself.
Only stopping so the driver
didn't have to do the paperwork.
What I leave unsaid,
is the look on her face
when she sees you
and knows
and you don't want to break her heart.
And what of how the wind pulls
you in if you stand too close.

CANON

And the smell of diesel exhaust at
60 miles per hour
is ineffable.

Haiku for My Fellow White People

Let those people speak.
Why don't you shut the fuck up,
then go punch Nazis?

Boketto

Lady liberty, trans woman,
sits on the cement banks of the Potomac.
In her left hand, cherry blossoms
from last year. She plucks one at a time
with her right, then tosses them
in the river. They ride the current
out of sight. Will she live to see
them bloom again?

A kerchief (from her murdered
sister justice's eyes)
pulled down over her nose and mouth,
keeps out tear gas from
containers behind her proudly made in USA.

A moment of doubt: should
she collect rocks in her pockets? Should
she fall into the water? Let her strength
seep away. Perhaps. But not today.

She stands, looks, crosses the street
unseen by police, walking home
to a small apartment far from K street,
far from Pennsylvania avenue,
far from the mall,
where she can get to work.

American Canon

Listener, I and I and we witness
the death of the American empire.
When it falls
it will be fast and sure.

We know why the caged child screams.
Ripped from parent's hands
by collaborators who cover their faces with hoods.

When America says to the universe, "Sir, I exist,"
the universe tells America to fuck off because she is
    pissed.

Two paths diverged in a wood,
and America traveled the one far too narrow
for everyone to fit.

They revel in freedom
for those who only desire the
freedoms
of whiteness
of straightness
of cisness.
But cheer, "We are free!
Do I contradict myself?
Very well then I contradict myself,
(I am large, I contain multitudes.)"

April is the cruellest month, breeding
hatred out of dead industry, mixing
false memory and desire, stirring
nostalgia with hate.
We measure our lives in Trump tweets and Senate votes;
fill up the phone lines
to beg Senators us to not kill us today.
Their staffers answer the phone,
"Dulce et decorum est pro patria mori."

Workers marched asleep. Many had lost their boots
But limped on, blood-shod, unable to pull themselves
by their own straps. They cannot hear their children ask
"Why the hole in the roof big enough
for me to fly out but the rain can get in?"

I, too, am America.
I take these words
–like others white me have
taken, co-opted
(even if they are part of me)–
and made them fit–
a stolen corset
shaping me
in a flattering light.

{ Lest though we think we are
kind [let us be
kind]
we should never forget [

never forget the smallpox blankets is one story among thousands never forget that we left queers in the concentration camps never forget we love celebrities more than our children { more than our little girls (more than our big girls) } never forget that AIDS was ignored never forget that we love our racist sexist homophobic xenophobic bigoted poets writers artists never forget the drug war is waged for discrimination never forget Stonewall was a riot never forget men with torches { tiki torches of all things (!) } marching never forget we invaded countries just because we could never forget he shits in a golden toilet never forget insulin used to be cheap never forget we can be hurt too never forget who cannot breathe never forget none of this happened long ago
never forget not
for guilt
but so we don't repeat
history
] that some
poets
were among the worst and }

JENDURBENT

Pull the stars from the American flag and
use bullets holes instead.
Our parents shot the american
dream long dead, left it
decomposing behind boarded windows
in redlined districts.

The bite
of the dog is fast.
And the cruelty
is the point.

America would not stop for history,
So she kindly stopped for us:
her barge contains forgotten glory,
oppression, ever broken trust.

We answered freedom's manifest destiny,
with flurries of bombs that would embarrass a blizzard.

We saw the best minds of our generation discarded be-
    cause of a man's career, starving hysterical men
    dragging themselves
in senate chambers prowling
& stalking
angry power.
Dark angel claims justice burning for the ancient con-
    nection to the fading dynamo in the machinery
    of democracy.

CANON

This generation greets death as an Internet friend
hugs and kisses and fucks and sweet oblivion.
We saw this coming.
We should have named our generation Cassandra–
we always saw this coming and they don't believe us.

The First Man I Loved

I fell in love with you as we ran
from the cops down alleyways.
When we finally stopped,
bent over,
hands on knees,
laughing, our trespasses
forgiven
misdemeanors in our minds.

The sunlight bleached
graffiti we tagged
years before,
on the then-new homes,
their erection postponed
by distant corporate
bankruptcy. The piles of dirt
left by unpaid contractors
littered with beer-can pull tabs
from long dead parties. They
poked out of the mud
like manicured fingernails.
We laughed. Our misdemeanors overshadowed
by fraud somewhere far away
in a shiny office building.

Even more years later, you got me high;
we watched shark week.
You rolled, you lit the shake again,
then passed it to me first.
I should have known the blank
eyes of a predator,
but I trusted you.
After you dosed me,
after you fucked me,
you took a shower while I cried.
You were
laughing, your trespass
no crime in your mind.

a dream of undoing

I was an 11 year old boy when I fell off my bike
jumping
over planks of wood
laid
across
bricks
scavenged
from alleyways.
from new construction, in lots recently made empty.

The falling never hurt.
The cut from a broken bottle I landed on [hands out (super hero)],
    didn't hurt.

Nothing hurt until the bike ride home, bleeding
bloody,
& broken,
and I didn't know if I would be beaten
or cared for.

As the doctor made rough handy work on my huge hands.
Chicks dig scars–he said, as he laced my hand like a sneaker.
Do they? I don't.
The pock marks on my face,
the scars on my knees from falling,
the cuts across my hands from stunts gone awry and washing hot
sinks full of half-sharp knives,

the slashes across my stomach and legs and arms I put there with
    purpose,
the scratches from cats (lest we forget them): chicks dig them?
Do they? Do we? Do I?
I do not. Not my own. No.
Later, the stitches from my life line
to my love line
perplexed the palmist in the family.

Maybe your scars tell a story of interest and intrigue,
    the time you fought a bear,
    the time you ran into a burning building,
    the time you got drunk and visited a body art parlor and saw
        a rose-petal scar on the artist, and you obsessed over your
        own de- sign until right as she branded you and you smelled
        the smell of the hot metal in your flesh and the smell of the
        hair on your arm burning.

But mine only
my clumsiness,
ineptitude: I cannot see
my skin as canvas of scars,
added by years, with the slow process of
a patient artist,
master of the most methodical methods.
I see only the failure
to know I would some day
be a 40 year old woman.
cupid bow.

CANON

"Tran Valentine's the name,
love and gender obfuscation is the game."
We live with
obsequious bottoms
and persnickety tops.
Bashful exhibitionists
and brash hidden lusts.

Please never forget
my siblings,
never ever forget,
you are wanted,
especially if you think so
and especially if you do not.

10 simple rules for dating a trans girl

Preface

Congratulations
your brand new trans
girlfriend does not come with
instructions, but
proper care of the trans girlfriend
may ensure a happy life
and maybe
a happy wife.

Also note individual variation
is part of the manufacturing process
and is not a bug
but a feature.

0

Trans women are women.

1

If you're a girl, dating her doesn't make you straight.
You don't lose your gold star–
you fucking cliche–
when her dick isn't made
of silicone.

If you're a straight boy, dating her doesn't make you gay.
Even if she comes in your mouth.
But beware,
we know how creepy you are.
We've seen some shit.

If you're bi or pan...we're cool.
Just remember:

2

Trans women are women.

3

You gotta tell her
that she's pretty.
And let her wear the thing
the girls wore in
high school.
She probably did not
go to high school as herself.
She was someone else:
Some sloppy nerd.
Some overwrought jock.
Someone else just because.
We're as varied as the men we never were.
She never had a girlhood
quite
like that.

4

She's gonna read the news
and about 30 times a year
a trans woman will be murdered in the United States.
Most of them will be women of color.
She will mourn
for her sisters
and she'll learn the dead girl's deadname from
the police statement to the paper
and she knows the guy who did it
will claim
he just
didn't
know
when he swiped left
on her tinder
and her profile read
"I'm trans,"
right there on the fucking top.

5

If you get her flowers,
she will cry.
And that's not a bad thing
she's had to learn that.
You should too.

6

Trans women are women.

7

Pickles.
I'm telling you pickles.
It's best to not explain.

8

I bet you thought I was gonna say trans women are women.
You know what: True! But
trans men are men and you better listen to our brothers,
And non-binary people are valid and good.

9

Muffing is a thing
you probably have never heard of
but you should find out with
ENTHUSIASTIC CONSENT!

10

And this is most important
Trans women are women.
Trans women are mothers
and sisters too.

If you can't tell, it's true.
And even if you can, it's true.
Please treat them right.
treat them like any other girl.
I hope mostly
that means you treat
all ladies well.
Trans women are friends
and lovers
and teachers
and co-workers too.

LGBTQuisling

There is a man who
betrays all he is
for a role.

His role is quisling.

He is the man married to the bigot.

He is the movie director ignoring trans women of color in history.

He is the man in drag who says "she mail" as a gag on TV.

The quisling is a bit of
self-important bullshit.

Whose "we gots" fester and pile up like a landfill of Styrofoam and
plastic bags and diapers

The quisling is the woman who thinks women is a womb, man.

The quisling is the friend who makes life harder
with free speech.

The quisling is me:
for my exhaustion,
for my ignorance,
for my am always
wrong and often
furiously

The quisling is the abuser.

The quisling is you. Because
in 100 years you
will never as good as you are
now.

And that is a beautiful thing.

xenoglossia (2018 rev)

Presented in many parts
—On Brueghel The Elder's "Tower of Babel" For R.A.W.: Fnord in Peace,
Brother Bob.

Warning: *This is a chain poem.*
Within the next 55 days you will receive
thirty-eleven-hundred pounds of chains.

Having conceived Babel, yet unable to build it themselves, they had thousands to build it for them. But those who toiled knew nothing of the dreams of those who planned. And the minds that planned the Tower of Babel cared nothing for the workers who built it.
—Maria (from Metropolis, 1927)

The theory seems to be that as long as a man is a failure he is one of God's children, but that as soon as he succeeds he is taken over by the Devil.
—H. L. Mencken

"There are no rules of architecture for a castle in the clouds."
—Gilbert K. Chesterton

Nihongo o hanashimasu ka

From scaffolds atop Babel I see gilded cities up
on the clouds, gorgeous gargoyles keeping watch over
the plains of Shinar, over us, over our
humble tower of rock and mud. On another horizon,
I can see the edge of the flat world, where water falls

into I don't know.

What grand architect drafted infinite tortoises on grid-
paper? Who conjures them from the four elements?
Who mixes fire and wood, draws ashen stains upon
their rocky backs like rugs? Who coalesces the jade
geodesic carapaces covering soupy-soft innards?

A clever eagle picks up a turtle and drops him from
such great heights onto rocks at the foot of our tower–
the eagle's meal workers envy, and steal and devour
and are happy, like the vultures of Babylon feasting on
infants dashed against the stones by water's edge.

I can see the bird's belly above me, down waving
like a holy flag after battle. Are eagles allowed
to see God when His own image remains blind to him?

I am cursed with a vision of Him, sitting in His
cloudy castle, moping and afraid of His creation.
We know He is an unknowable deity behind walls,
a petty deity who delays coming to see us,
an impotent deity who status we will conquer
with rocks and muddy masonry.

I am alone within sight of God's flying buttresses
and below is firmament and my fellow man. Alone,
against orders, I climbed atop and away from it all,
to see all creation; I could splash like the son
of Daedalus, barely a ripple on the Aegean, arms

splayed; a plucked, panicked, clumsy albatross, flapping
against nothing. The castle would stand unmoved.

¿Usted habla español?

Near the quarry, the king no longer hears our words,
his words are no longer the words of our fathers and
father's fathers. He speaks in gibberish and nonsense:
the talk of animals rather than men. Is the king mocking me?
I compliment his robes and he mocks me? The other men look
confused, like fish getting clubbed on the pier; they are
out of their element and facing violencia rhetorica.

What is this? We've labored at the bottom of this
tower for years, our reward stripped with no possibility
of ascension. We, the many, the soldiers, the workers,
the collective hive buzzing at his needs with our next
meal, our next rest, our next apotheosis.

What is the order, sir? Nonsense! Nonsense? More taxes?
Speaking in tongues and illiterate lips? No chief of state!
No-one can respect the red robe and crown with no mind,
the body that holds them both trembles like a beaten bitch
babbling and incoherent. The soldiers talk all at once,
no-one listening. Us workers either. We do not understand
any. There is no coup, no conspiracies, no beyond our words.
We all speak louder, maybe volume is comprehension.

Self-perpetuating autocracy to mindless anarchy,
everyone with their own mistaken identity. I will head

home, south, down the Tigris, to Ur, and see my wife
and children, nurse them with tales of woe and my small
farm, but do they know my language? Can I show them
how to plow fields and how to raise barns?

Can I show them my scars and tell my war stories,
exaggerated and full of meaning like my fathers?
Slaves scatter like moonlight in the clouds, and last
I see of the king is a stomped-on collar, the white
of that hare is absolutely meaningless to anyone
without the words–

Sprechen Sie Deutsch?

This hero is the last one on the shore at the foot
of Babel, my leg dangling off the pier, schools
of fish just below. God is behind him, a slight
glow of wisdom and practiced senses of the soldier
feels the presence, that final visitation.
"The fire of his opal eyes making glowing, living
jewels, measure steadily." The soldier's song:

"The purpose of this is resonant and crystal,
like air in its transparency. What is your reason
for fear? What does it mean to you if we the people
Say 'let there be light?' and take your place on our
own Olympus? What is your damage? Your malfunction,
imperfect creator? And what does it say about
your creation, the strongest of the animals?
What of your disinformation and glossolalia spread

From horizon to horizon?" The soldier continues:

"Who hears me among the ranked angels as I
cry out? The one with twelve wings, the snake
in our garden, our creation-right, and he helps us
break your ignorance spell, the snake is our savior,
knowledge over good and evil. Now, we ascend, we
approach you and now, here, God, what have you given
us? New definitions for old concepts; contemptuous!
What is your fear?" He breathes deep and starts again:

"Take this as prophecy: We will not end here.
This tower dwarfs you, and towers of the future
will look down in disdain at the clouds, and the
round world below will be a pale blue dot."

Ĉu vi parolas Esperanton?

Let me tell you the story of all the monsters of all time.
In the beginning was the word, struck one letter at a time
with an old typewriter, or a pen so cheap and dry you can hear
the scratch of the ball-point rolling in-socket, reaching up
into the well to bring more ink to the page. This word
was composed next to thousands of others; and lined up
in neat rows like soldiers razing a village, collecting slaves
to build great works and be lost and forgotten in Moloch's name.

The sun is setting, and I stand in the penumbra of the tower
which stretches across the world to where the sun will rise.

How many rooms are within the tower? As many rooms as years
	remain.
Did you think we made it to confuse the god Loki? No. What a pitiful
Man. We took his daughter and confounded so she could not escape
and instead did our bidding for our worship. Because the best way
To kill a god is to not believe in him. Hel, Loki's lovely daughter
was not always confined to shadow her blue-black face. She is not
all she seems. She desires her own worship, and through the roots
of Yggdrasil, she found her place. Demeter did not search long
for her daughter. Do you believe me? You need not. Someone will.

Bullshit makes flowers grow and that is beautiful.

Have our endless doors made you a rube? Cube after cube
separated by endless arches. I have the path. Pay me. There
is no minotaur, scraping his axe against the walls,
alighting stars into existence. No monster mumbles,

"Let there be . . . LET there be . . . LET there BE. . . "

Unazungumza Kiswahili?

"Since Noah's flood we have become brothers again,"
I said to the man before the confusion of his tongue
(because I surely was not the confused one).
He gently teased me and said those were the floods of
Ogygian. Regardless, the antediluvian times was a long
ago past. After we worked we went to his house in the
shadow of the tower, that rounded ziggurat against
the sky. We laid on his roof and looked up in vertigo

CANON

as the clouds passed what was the top of the tower;
small chunks of sky were consumed by scaffolds
ladders, and levers. We enjoy the silence.

When the stars came out, he opened his mouth on me
and I understood as if his words were my own. We traded
words over tea overflowed with milk and honey. Oh!
We were not united any differently than in your bed.

Later, after we lay in bed breathing softly
near one another, his chest hair under my hand,
we laid in silence. Until I broke it:

"Our words are the words of Adam, and he
named all things, and that makes him a kind
of god." I said this without fear. He nodded, "Eden
is our creation-right. Together, we will smash
the flaming swords that guard its entrance;
we will pass through the valley. We'll eat fruits
and taunt the serpents and claim what is our own."

When we looked up again at the stars, we drew
lines between them with our fingers and named
the constellations as if it were the first time,
As if we were Adam. Sometime after Scorpio,
he spoke pointing upward at empty space
and was as if my ears were filled with water.

Badakizu euskaraz?

There is an obelisk at the forest edge, the clump of black
combines with the trees against the dawn sky; ebon veins
flow out like the fine blue ones of my forearm. Villagers
and slaves like me crowd around it and tilt their heads
as if we were confused dogs, as if we understand this
as more than the block of rock.

This is a moment of evolution; the obelisk was the first
firmament, appeared again when Cain slew Abel, when Adam
begat Eve, and when we find one on the moon, believe
our footprints aren't alone in the dust of this planet.

We all see the monolith as a prize, some solver of all.
Merchants see it is a profit. And when a stonecutter
puts his chisel against the rock and raises his hammer,
suddenly there is nothing there but the dew-wet black
forest, moist, like cake, and a heavy hammer pulled back
left in the dirt, grass returning to form where its owner
once stood, and then no more. Yes! I ran away.

Parlez-vous français?

I address the dirt, my dirt, for I am the king of Babylon!

"Did your ancestors tell you to play with your creation
like mashed potatoes and gravy volcanoes? Disaster
is not a plaything, malevolent entity. Beautiful
volcanoes will not create enlightenment. Giant bivalves

may be amusing, but do not necessarily create the most valuable pearls. Let us pry them apart to inspect them, let us pry the rocks up from the quarries, slabs of Earth held aloft in arches masoned by triumphant mud. For what is mud but where dirt meets water. Even a fool knows this!

"Adam told his son, Seth, that Eve and Adam were born of dirt. When I die–when I am fully grown–I will return to dirt. It doesn't take a genius to know Adam and Eve and Seth are here in the walls of this building, at the base of all that is holy, of all the world.

"Adam had his own Babel, sowed his own confusion, when he came from the garden, he changed the languages of all the animals; so the cat attacks the mouse. As above, so below."

I lie. That is what I would have said if I had the words, instead I merely said, "I should have been a mason."

Você fala português?

I lie because I lie. I write because I lie. And that all is a lie and I don't know why I tell them. Did I fail you. Though I know it's not a test this time. I told my mother I didn't believe in you, reader, and she wept for my eternal soul. Though that is a lie, too. But that is a mother's lie. There is no soul. Father taught me that.

Lie. Prophesy. The difference is the arrangement of

tea leaves. I will tell you the first human clone
will be Adam, and he will be perfect in every way,
like all children.

He will proceed with us through that window like a bullet
-back and to the left-and the tower of hell and the great
serpentines of the highest order. He will stray far
from the ivory tower to a the cusp of the forest
garden where snakes bloom and flowers flow and take
his place where he belongs.

The star anise is in season. May it bring us all
bitterness! Behold the mountain we made at Babel!
As the once and future Adam watches, it trembles
crumbles. The sentence for hubris is-

Do you speak English?

I'm sorry; I've been drinking. Send money. I can't order
beer or wine any longer. So I just drink whatever is left
in the ashtrays when the bar closes.

The universe is a big place, maybe even the biggest. On this round
world we're scattered, with continents linked by dinosaur bones,
raindrops
looking to join rivers looking to join rivers looking to join oceans.

Can you find you, among masses of men pouring out? Dirty
water and you dilute you, you think. No! You become more. You are
the earth plus plastic! You are mere tools to give me what I need.

CANON

Have I found the god in everything who makes the grass green?
It ain't Eris. That bitch and her golden apple have nothing on me.

Mu is the answer. Says little,
does less,
means nothing.

Are you looking at
the trees? Only you can prevent
forest fires. Smokey will just steal your pic-a-nic basket.

Or is that me?

Let that motherfucker burn, leave landscape like a body builder's muscles standing in relief. Can we laugh at them? Do they even lift, brother? Let the handlebar mustaches catch their tears.

Buddha put down his pen and crossword and told you
not to worry, madness and vexation
would be your reward
if we contemplate the beginning. The beginning does not lead anywhere useful.

Except the end. Can't? Or? Infinity!

You will build broken cathedrals and worship plastic refrigerator magnets.

As you are outside yourself, reader, you promote you to godhood.
You are knowing more than the you seem.
come with me and step toward omniscience.

JENDURBENT

printf("tlhIngan Hol Dajatlh'a'" && eggplant_emoji);

Reader, contemplate:
the usefulness of
the little chip-clip as-seen-on-TV.

Thusly, from cans of meat electric this way came:
disclaims most old of our liability taste
it also wave tells you
how conversation between Captain Helding
and high-jump dragon boat
festival of your husband–all decoration
a man came and was favourable:
and the real green-eyed monster Hungarian
with graffito satisfaction that showed itself.

And when mutton makes sense as a cake topping,
next to man and man, man and wife, wife and wife
and everyone in between and without and outside the false di-
      chotomy of gender
and then even more
and undreamed plural singularities
That will be the day we understand universal grammar,
and we all know that merciful Cthulu,
King Kong,
and Frankenstein
died for your sins.

Do I speak English?

The emoji and Latin and the French and the affectation of ironic hate and
all all all the words that could exist.
We no longer build do we? Did we ever though, really?
Didn't cross-bound cardinals chastise their children for staring at
 the
stars
and dreaming of anything?

And all this–
dear god,
all this–
for a question
from a child
on a picture
on a wall
of a story
from a book–
and a god–
I can't believe in.

Storming the Foothills of Mount Olympus

1.

All you need know: I am a soldier, dressed in a prior hoplisis,
fighting against the gods. My goals: succor and gold.

Achlys moves the Earth with her words: "Armies
onward towards the crest of this hill and
onward towards the home of the Gods;
ever forward, forward to usurp these
faulty idols. We do not pray, we demand
what's ours and will raze their castles to sand."

I say, "Those who stopped just before this hubris
are what we call, 'Unambitious.' They are
forgotten soldiers who history clods
upon with terrible hooves. Great people: this
is how we inhabit history. With ideas and tar
and mortar and art. We are dancing stars."

—We are not the greatest. We would fall
under the forgotten tasks of our ancestors.—

Achlys orders us further upwards to lay siege
the Home of the Gods. We will starve
them of pomegranate and catapult rocks
and rotten meat. We will not leave these

mountains without just rewards, riches carved
by Zeus; his burdens become our toy models.

I can see the great walls now: battlements
bare of soldiers are covered with a haze—
a smoke that refuses to rise. It is dusk;
I lay my head on the grass; slaves raise tents
for officers. I breathe deep: their supper today
is fowl: all save the best officers have gluttonous ways.

The soldiers empty stomachs churn, prolapse into
nightmares and make sleep exhausting.

Morning. "Xolotl has distemper; the eagle god's soft eggs
poach well," Achlys tells us we will be upon them,
we will fight the gods and triumph and win and reclaim
"For we have made them in natures image, the hags
and the dogs and the eagles and warriors!" Then
she stops short, breathes deep, and pulls up phlegm.

She spits on the ground; it is clear and healthy.
"We spit upon their throne; we deny their place
at the head of our lives; we deny them any fame
or hope or existence. These gods—never the
way to truth—have occluded our search, face
to face they tell us that we're the inferior race."

My own doubts are still full and fast. There might
be something to this even still, even still.

CANON

"They're worse than us because they learn slowly;
even now, we see that bombs and wrath are tools
of last resort, and they act like the unwashed.
They are not our betters. We raid brutally
but with hope. We will kill those fools
who, with our sacrifices, lived petty & fought petty duels.

"And we see their castles brick by brick now,
each one white square and arranged by a slave.
Imagine such a life! An eternity of toil for naught;
for the mere pleasure of an ungrateful sow.
Zeus is mine. When I enter His castle, I'll pave
the world with his soldiers, from general to knave."

—Do her slaves hear her words as she promised freedom?
Do they know she lies like every man before her? No.—

Small men—advisors—scurry about. Taking news
from scouts and prisoners returned. "Silence,
silence!" she says, wills, orders. "Speak, men
in chains! What returned treasures from our dues
to the gods lie ahead? How shall we battle? Lance,
sword, or siege?" Them: "There is barely even a fence.

When we ran to the gates and throw them agape—
no longer afraid of terrible white towers & buttresses
overhead," he said, "We scurried, looking to pillage, ran
upwards, forever upwards, into empty spires. From nape
to foundation, of goods or gods or men." "What nemesis
bound you, stripped you, and held you in place?"

JENDURBENT

—When gods are gone, who else is left? Who remains to lock
them up? Logic says themselves, but it is a cause for wonder.—

"Achlys, we locked ourselves in the dungeon and traded
our freedom for fear of blasphemy. We were not afraid
of gods but certainly of no deity. Let us return to our holes,
bound and miserable and secure." She looks over faded
skin, gaunt and hanging loose, and clothes frayed,
worn. She says, "Do you say that when we raid

we, too, will feel this fear, and feel an ache for restraint?"
"Mayhap." "Well," she says, "I have felt deep aches, though
I wouldn't call them aches from fear." We laugh. "Souls,"
she says, after the slow men understand her faint
wit, "take a boat to that river and row, quickly, row.
Stay midriver. Rocks line the shores. Beware of undertows."

—Of course you don't know (do they?) just around
the bend and below waterfalls and rocks and hard clay.—

2.

Awake again. Unlike in my dream, there was no maiden;
only a pile of urine-soaked hay. I regret nothing.

"Our Queen!" someone yells, "The Queen is dead! Smothered
under feathered pillows, her last breath still warm on silk
pillow cases. Will you, can you, may you not weep, sweet
Achlys is dead. Some pious bastard, some fervent brother
of some false prophet, some demon or another of it's ilk

stole the life of her who led us to the honey and milk."

I ask, "Guards?! Where were the guards? All her guards
in this world were as impotent djinni on a vacuous moon.
Dead by dawn; her life disappeared before birds tweet.
Dead. Now, only by tall tale and legend will mere bards
finish her deeds. She is dead, gone too soon, too soon.
Now our own quests look just as quashed and doomed."

The others rise from their beds, find our leader vanquished,
and merely shrug and turn toward home. Honorless fools.

"You cowards evacuate even before a funeral dirge reverbs
through this valley," I yell. "Very well! I shall go alone
against the gods. Your leader dies, you run! I won't abandon
this war. You, who would simply turn away, are the turds
a skunk would not bury! You could not present a bone
even for a siren!" Abandoned, I bury her on my own.

So I set myself with a grimace upon the burial of my queen,
I took a shovel left by a gravedigger (profiteers,
but I don't envy their task) and planted rocky dirt one
pile on another, down until the ground was unseen
even if I stretched up on my toes. The grave clear
and deep and long: I climbed out, thirsty for wine or beer.

I do not pray. No gods remain to hear my cries. Yes!
I mourn but I will not pray. And I do drink deep.

At the end of the day, she lies still under dirt and rocks
and some pitiable headstone, and I alone sit here. Even

JENDURBENT

the supply train is out of sight, now. It is just me
and that pitiable, terrible, white castle, its loch
choked with algae. Dusk erupts, and some un-heavenly
light flickers from the building. There is no decision

I have made so willingly, to head into that abode to slay
whatever demons, gods, or men that killed or ordered
to kill my queen. Thusly and forever, I shall forsake the
minor desires of life and love, and my thoughts every day
will be revenge for matricide and execution of brutal cowards.
I know and ignore that such vengeance makes hearts sour.

Sustain me, Vengeance. I cannot plead with an emotion,
but may it sustain me for what is surely a forever war.

I sleep again after burying my queen, and I hold no hope
the night will slacken my rage, but it turned inward.
How dare I—all hubris and fantasy—make justice? I
shame at the false words I said. I fashion a rough rope
into a loose noose and think. I am not a bard,
I am a fool who makes love sword-in-scabbard

and I am a fool who cannot finish even a fool's errand.
How dare I—all failures in my crowded heart—propose
anything but to dive from cliff to rocks. Why try?
Let me do nothing and not fail rather than to defend
some concept as honor, valor, pride. I can say to those
who doubt me, "I am a coward, written in poetry or prose."

But am I? I have lived through more battles

CANON

than memories. I know there is valor in beer!

I face the castle and eye its iron fence and surrounding
curtilage, again the grounds look idle, not gardener nor
soldier disturb the architecture, glamorous white
stones stacked and grouted with more glittering
mortar disturbed regularly with murder holes, no door
visible. This is more keep then castle; a fortress for war

and no other purpose. Fear not, we are at the foothills
of the great mountains, and this keep is but the first
building to fall. "Coward," I tell myself, "before the light
dims in the sky, add at least one number to your kills."
I breathe, close my eyes, and when I open the curse
of fear has cleared and I move to slake my murderous thirst.

The distance collapses as I approach, alone, but the sun
sets fast in the sky. Wasn't it morning not long ago?

The dark is no matter for this mission, and there is no restraint
upon my violence with what I find on the throne. I'll run though
that false idol with my bare hands, and the pitiable souls
he's deceived will then be free. The hope and the light is faint,
I charge closer to this castle, this keep, into the row upon row
of gleaming white bricks towering over the moat's deadly under-
    tows.

There it is! A massive door, and I must enter it. Ground traded
grass for rock in front of that door—and yes, yes I am afraid.
Solid! Cut from one tree two men's height wide. I see no holes,

for keys nor hands. I push against where the wood is faded,
and it moves easily, and I can imagine ropes, frayed
with time, pulling it open. I step in, ready to begin my raid—

The sword is comfortable in my hand, and the shield offers
comfort like a mother. I press forward, ever forward.

3.

The smell is wet and cold and tired, like boots
worn walking through a shallow runoff in the early Spring.

Of course it is dank and dark and dirty, what clean world
do I expect in a castle built for war? I must confess a fear
of bugs bigger than my hand. An unlit torch in its holder
smells of pitch and tar, so I spark my knifes whorled
Damascus blade against the wall and light it. A small tear
of flame falls to the floor. I piss it out with my mourning beer.

I belch. After the echo, no sound other than distant droplets
of some unknown liquid and the crackling flame. The corridor
branches: two paths diverge and I turn left, opposite a dead cur's
pile accompanying quiet flies. "And this fecund waste, wet
with maggots, is found in a castle? Even disgust in war
is a weapon," and I trudge onward, but I need not travel far.

{ When two gods meet, nude as the barbarous men who
made them, each believes they are the higher rank. }

The walls widen into a room, the ceiling high, peaked
and adorned with a story of creation. A single man sits,

cross-legged, center of the room, looking at me curiously,
floating. I can smell his vanity from here, the stink
of his perfumed self offending even beyond the dog shit
I avoided; his face tells me he's not long from mommy's tit.

"I am all that is man and god," he says. I respond, "Obesity
should not be a goal of an immortal." The portly hovering
man smiles. "Ah. Your joke is unfunny, old, and simply
louder. Originality is not your generation's forte. Pity.
to waste immortality on a normal person, not a king
or someone worth any more than a strand of string."

Either the floor is warped, or my eyes are. Light or this man
play tricks! I trust this man even less than light and shadow.

I charge the floating prophet and knock him from mirrorwork.
And, sprawled out on the cobbled stones and dirt, white
clothes turn dingy gray as he fumbles to his feet.
"You fool! What curses you engender! Go on, smirk
now, but know," he inhales sharply, "I am surely in the right.
You are damned to eternal life, no Godesses lighten

your load. Your friends—" "I have none!" "—they die in fires.
When the world ends you exist. No man shall end you, fool.
Even death may die before you have a chance to meet
your end. You will wish, beg, plead for your own funeral pyre!
Even upon grass that could be put out with a baby's drool,
but no. You will live forever, even past the sun grows cool."

JENDURBENT

I laughed just now, unable to keep it away. Tell a sadistic soldier like me I'll live forever and see how wretched that forever is.

"Very well; I am immortal, and only God can end this life," I laugh again, "I will gain honor! And how does prophecy change me? I fight for my queen's memory and her whispered sighs live beyond your lie-strewn oaths!" He says, "Strife will be your life and her memory down the bowels of history. She will be forgotten by everyone, even you eventually."

"As long as I live, I will speak her name." "And even the air will be gone around you, and your voice will make no sound." "I will write her words," I say. He contends, "The ink will blur among all the words of humanity. But to be just a little fair, some writings will live until even the tablets of stones are ground into powder, just before the sun grows plump, red, and round."

I say, "You say the sun cools, then you say it reddens and grows. You fool!" He says, "You are a fool. Stars live long lives."

He sighs and rolls his head around his shoulders, and I hear his bones crack. He stands. "Tell me what you fear." Again, I laugh, "Have you considered writing comedies?" He coldly reads me, "You fear the terrible enlightening knowledge. Fear knowing I am truthful and right. Maybe just then, at the end of this world, when neither kith nor kin

surround you...Tell me, how is your mother's back? Her other pains?" "How do you know of my mother?" I ask. "Well, I could never know, except you told me.

CANON

You told me of your mother, your family, your pack
of wolf-dogs raised since pups to be loyal to no other.
Even I doubted. Until your torch lit this foggy ether."

"You could have guessed all of those things. Tell
me more about what you know of my mother."

"Her back is twisted like a screw. She worked for your
gain while your father warred under your forgotten queen."
I raise my hand, "I would not—" "—say such things if
I were you?" he cut me off, knowing my words before I do.
"You will learn much, immortal one, though she seems
great right now, her existence is as ephemeral as steam."

"Despicable or ephemeral? Choose one!" I say. "Both,"
he says, "Evil and good are simple words, you teach this
to all the children and monsters of our time; when a whiff
of an errant wind could kill you, every day is a trophy
to be held and cherished and every night's sleep is bliss."
He smiles, "My words are weak; my argument is amiss.

"I will show, not tell," he says. "I was once like you. The only
way out is through." He disappears, and I am again war torn.

To be continued "When It's Done."

Afterword

I wish I was a better poet.

That's it.

I wish that when I feel the compulsion (and, dear reader, do I feel that particular word to do things with words, that what I made seemed important and good. But it never does. It never will. Regardless of what I think of the poems, I hope you like them. I hope that you find something enjoyable in them. I hope there is a turn of phrase that brings you joy, an image that touches you, or maybe a sentence that makes you feel a little less alone in the universe.

I just hope…and that, in and of itself, is new for me.

I love you. No matter who you love or what body you inhabit.

Thank you for reading.

About the author

Jen Durbent is a non-binary transgender woman-type thing who lives in the greater Chicagoland area with her family. Jen uses she, they, or it pronouns. She also performs stand-up comedy and is working on her second novel and screenplay. Find her at jendurbent.com and on the Facebook, Instagram, Twitter, and so on as JenDurbent

Selected works

Sexts and Sonnets (Poems, 2017, Self Published)
My Dinner with Andrea (Novel, 2018, from HYBRID Ink)

About the publisher

HYBRID Ink, LLC began in 2018 with it's inaugural publication, Jen Durbent's *My Dinner With Andrea*. Borne out of a desire to see more of the publications they loved, Madison Scott-Clary and the editors at HYBRID Ink made it their goal to provide well-versed and sophisticated works of fiction, poetry, and creative non-fiction.

We want writing that gets us thinking about ourselves, stories that span genres, and words that change the way we look at the world.